I0476763

ISBN-13: 978-1523474721

ISBN-10: 1523474726

Lee Li Lian

dedicated to ...

This is for the many insurance sales agents I have trained and crossed paths with. Thank you for sharing with me the countless challenges, joy and satisfaction that you have faced in your businesses. Thank you for giving me the strength to carry on training, writing and inspiring.

This is also for the many awesome ex-colleagues I have had in Great Eastern Life Singapore. Thank you for the trust, team work and empathy we have shown to one another. We always had one another's backs.

Lee Li Lian

AcknowledgeMent

"We must find time to stop and thank the people who make a difference in our lives" – John F. Kennedy

I wish to personally thank the following people for their contributions to my inspiration and knowledge and other help in creating this book:

1. My husband, Koh Chee Koon, whose encouragement and support gave me the strength to complete this book.

2. Mr Philip Png, ex-colleague, for the research we have done together when we started developing a curriculum on this.

3. Mr Mervyn Chew, ex-boss, for his advice and trust which gave me the confidence to do what I do best.

WHY POWER PHRASES?

Power phrases are used to **emotionalize** a sale. It is about saying something in a short and sweet manner, enhanced with key words that will deeply impact your clients' thinking.

Power phrases add punch to a line or a paragraph and it's usually use to start off a sentence or close a sale. It also helps to stimulate one's mind to think and answer the question that was being asked.

To make power phrases powerful, you got to read it over and over again. This is essential so that you can apply them anytime, anywhere and recite it with ease, proper pronunciation, pauses and confidence. ***Know them well*** so that you will not hesitate while using it in order to use it effectively.

Too often in business, we choose the wrong words, say the wrong things and eventually send the wrong message causing the sale to be jeopardized. This handbook provides you with 100 ***simple yet impactful*** phrases to start off with. Choose the ones that you really like and feel most comfortable with; modify it to fit your style.

Say What You Mean, Mean What You Say, & Get What You Want!

100 POWER PHRASES

01.   Insurance is purchased not because somebody must die, but because others must live!

02.   Will you enjoy retirement, or retire from enjoyment?

03.   Money is both difficult to earn and keep.

04.   Money cannot buy love but love can buy money.

05.   If you cannot save money to buy Life Insurance, then you have to buy Life Insurance to save money.

06.   Won't you agree that a widow is not nearly as concerned about receiving 'inflated' or 'deflated' dollars as she is about receiving enough dollars?

07.   Life Insurance is the only way that people can make their Wills before they make their money.

08.   The more you are worth, the more your children stand to lose. The less you are worth, the less they can afford to lose.

09. To buy Life Insurance, you need the willingness to give up something today so that your family won't have to give up everything tomorrow.

10. The only thing worse than a home without a mother is a mother without a home.

11. You would certainly give your life for your children, so why not insure it for them?

12. If you're having a tough time getting by on your salary now, how well do you think your family will get by without it?

13. Life Insurance won't keep you from dying, but it will keep your family's plans from dying with you.

14. A man's widow is unprepared to live if he is financially unprepared to die.

15. Life Insurance is not an added obligation; it's the best way to meet the obligations that you already have.

16. $500 a month is worth more to a widow than $1500 a month is worth to a wife.

17. You can't solve a permanent problem with temporary insurance.

18. No man plans to be poor when he reaches retirement; the trouble lies in not planning to avoid being poor.

19. The size of your paycheck has increased dramatically in the last 10 years. But is it any easier now to accumulate money than it was 10 years ago?

20. The difference between an old man and an elderly gentlemen is an adequate monthly income.

21. You can't plan your future in the future – you have to plan it now.

22. We owe our parents at least enough to pay for your cost of dying and leave them financially even with the world.

23. It takes a smart young man to take care of the old man you will be someday; and the only money you can depend on when you get

there is what you send ahead while you are young right now.

24. I agree that the economy is uncertain. That's the very reason most people have an insurance program. If we could be certain of everything we wouldn't need insurance – isn't that true?

25. Do you know that 90% of your assets are standing in your shoes right now?

26. 1 ordinary father is able to support 4 children, but it takes 4 extraordinary children to support 1 disabled father.

27. If you get sick or hurt and cannot work, there are 4 sources of income for your family:

Relatives, Friends, Charity and Insurance. Which do you prefer?

28. The Titanic was supposed to be unsinkable – but it still had lifeboats.

29. I know you have insured your life; have you insured your living?

30. When people reach retirement, they are either very glad they bought Life Insurance or very sorry they didn't.

31. There is no finer asset at age 65 than an income you cannot outlive.

32. There is nothing more certain than death, and nothing more certain than Life Insurance.

33. Many investments ask for a dollar and promise pennies; Life Insurance asks for pennies and promises dollars.

34. Life Insurance is like a parachute – if you ever need it and don't have it, you will never need it again.

35. Death comes every day to someone and someday to everyone.

36. When you die, the bank gives your loved ones what you have saved; the insurance company pays your loved ones what you meant to have.

37. The Greek philosopher Plato once said, 'Death is certain; but the moments and timings of death are uncertain.'

38. You can say, 'I don't need it', but can you say 'my family won't need it'?

39. More good things are lost by indecision than by wrong decision, aren't they?

40. I cannot accept your apology for not buying because I am not the beneficiary; your apology should be directed to your wife and children, Mr. Prospect.

41. Someone always pays for Life Insurance, whether a man buys or not; the question is, who pays? ….. The man or the family?

42. The difference between the old man and an elderly gentleman is a decent income during retirement.

43. Wives may not believe in Life Insurance, but widows always do.

44. Have you ever met a widow who complained that her husband had too much Life Insurance?

45. Life Insurance is the only instrument that will generate a known sum at an unknown time.

46. If you wouldn't like to live the rest of your life on the face amount of your present

insurance, how do you expect your wife to?

47. Losing a father is bad enough, inheriting a part time mother makes it
worse, doesn't it?

48. You can put me off, but you can't put your competitors off – death and disability.

49. It isn't easy to be old or poor, but it's a great deal worse to be both.

50. Just because you stop working doesn't mean you stop loving your wife, children and grandchildren. That's why you need permanent Life Insurance, isn't it?

51. No person ever dies at the right time, do they?

52. A person may use credit to live, but their family needs cash when they die, don't they?

53. You may last longer than your money.

54. No debt should last longer than the person who created it, should it?

55. Your wife should be left something that will take care of her – not something she will take care of, shouldn't she?

56. 'NO' has always been the first two letters of 'nothing', I have never liked what 'nothing' implies. Would I be right in

assuming that you do not like the meaning of 'NO' either?

57.   In the final analysis, all you can leave your wife with is 'dignity of choice' isn't it?

58.   If you had a goose that laid golden eggs, would you insure the eggs or the goose that laid them?

59.   If you can save as much money in the next five years as you have in the last five years, will you be satisfied?

60.   Sometimes the biggest price you pay in the world is doing nothing. A lot of people did nothing wrong; they just do nothing. That's what's wrong?

61. If your partner dies or becomes permanently disabled, how long would you be willing to do 100% of the work for 50% of the profits?

62. If it were free how much insurance would you like?

63. Do you know anyone who has died who had too much insurance?

64. If you were to die because of someone else's negligence, how much would you want your family to sue for? Should they have any less if you die by other means?

65. You and wife together can handle debt, but can she handle debt herself?

66. A Life Insurance person brings no financial problem to any prospect, they only bring the solutions.

67. If every wife knew what every widow knows, every husband would be insured for more, wouldn't they?

68. If you suffered a critical illness or serious accident would you sooner lose your home or your mortgage?

69. Do you have a family debt extinguisher fund?

70. If you weren't here, who would you want to ask take care of your obligations?

71. What assets are instantly created for your family and estate if you die?

72. Which is harder for a widow? Being unprepared or being unfunded?

73. We don't have a choice about good luck or bad luck, do we? It just happens?

74. How would your family be affected if you couldn't work for 2 years?

75. Will you be leaving your family with assets or liabilities?

76. Are you aware that your children stand to lose two parents if your partner is forced to go back to work after the death of a spouse?

77. Your family's outcome relies on your income.

78. Saving your life shouldn't mean losing your savings.

79. Income Protection benefits are Dollars of Dignity. They mean not having to beg, not having to rely on charity, not having to borrow, not sending your spouse out to work, not having to sell off your assets, and not having to downgrade your lifestyle.

80. Comparing the number of doctors to the number of undertakers in the phone book, will give you an indication of the number of unwell people requiring attention compared to

the lesser number of deaths requiring attention.

81.　You are aware that the biggest gamble your spouse and family can ever take is on you. Why not minimize the risk with an income protection plan?

82.　Did you know there are two ways to make money? People at work and money at work. To have both is better, isn't it?

83.　You have an Accountant and a Solicitor, but do you have anyone whose responsibility it is to deliver money in the event of a death, disability or long-term illness?

84. Cancer need not kill, the lack of money will.

85. When a person dies, his income 'dies' and his expenses 'die' as well. If he doesn't die, his income 'dies' but his expenses go up!

86. The premium is not the problem; the premium is the solution to the problem.

87. Life Insurance is a shield to meet the blow that you can't see it coming.

88. Which amount would you prefer to pay? A small known amount or a big unknown amount?

89. Disability would need much more money than death.

90. The asset that you are creating through your various insurance policies could ironically become your liability if you have not insure your insurance.

91. Invest in yourself and your future!

92. I hope that you fall into the category that I can speak to.

93. How would you like an account that allows you to create your wealth before saving towards it?

94. Do you know that the power of compounding is the 8th wonder of the world?

95. You do not buy life insurance policy; you buy an education for

the kids, a lifetime income for your spouse, a pension for an old person. You buy peace of mind, happiness and contentment when you buy life insurance.

96. You say you have trouble living within your income – consider living without your income.

97. You finish the job if you live, we finish the job for you if you die, become disabled or long term sick.

98. Whatever reason you may have for not starting this plan now will only sound ridiculous to your widow.

99.   You got to get it when you don't
       want it so that you have it when
       you need it.

100.   Whatever the dollar's future
       value, the man who has one will
       be better off than then man who
       doesn't.

ABOUT LEE LI LIAN

Li Lian is a certified Trainer in the area of continuing education and training. She has been actively involved in the Insurance industry for more than a decade. She had learned and gained many insightful experiences from working with fellow colleagues, financial planners and industrial leaders. She is also a Master Trainer in Professional Pattern of Management for Kinder Brothers International.

Li Lian graduated from Ngee Ann Polytechnic Singapore in 1999 where she majored in Business Studies. She went on to pursue a Bachelor's Degree with Curtin University of Technology in Australia, majoring in Sales & Marketing.

Li Lian is also a Singapore Politician and a former Member of Parliament, representing the single

member constituency of Punggol East. She
ventured into politics in the year 2006 when her
husband brought her to a political rally. Since
then she dedicated much of her time to
volunteerism. She has helped out in numerous
grassroots activities which includes helping needy
families, etc In 2013, she was elected by the
people to represent them in Punggol East SMC
via a By-Election.

Li Lian is happily married with a daughter.
During her free time, she enjoys singing and
dancing with her daughter.

www.ingramcontent.com/pod-product-compliance
Lightning Source LLC
Chambersburg PA
CBHW061237180526
45170CB00003B/1330